Kindfulness

kindfulness

AJAHN BRAHM

Wisdom

Wisdom Publications
199 Elm Street
Somerville, MA 02144 USA
wisdompubs.org

Library of Congress Cataloging-in-Publication Data
Names: Ajahn Brahm, 1951– author. | Bartok, Josh, editor.
Title: Kindfulness / Ajahn Brahm ; edited by Josh Bartok.
Description: Somerville : Wisdom Publications, 2016.
Identifiers: LCCN 2015023641 | ISBN 1614291993 (pbk. : alk. paper)
Subjects: LCSH: Buddhist meditations. | Kindness—Religious aspects—Buddhism.
Classification: LCC BQ5572 .A53 2016 | DDC 294.3/4435—dc23
LC record available at http://lccn.loc.gov/2015023641

ISBN 978-1-61429-199-2   ebook ISBN 978-1-61429-216-6

20 19 18 17 16   5 4 3 2

Cover design by Phil Pascuzzo. Interior design by Gopa & Ted2, Inc.
Set in Village Roman 9.8/16.

Table of Contents

Preface

AN ANCIENT TEACHING SAYS that by looking after oneself, one looks after others—and by
looking after others, one looks after oneself.
Kindfulness, the subject of this small book, is a
wonderful way to bring this truth into our lives.

Through stories and direct instruction, I'll
introduce you to kindfulness and teach you a
powerful method of being kindfully present to
what I call "the beautiful breath." This practice unfolds gradually over time, and I'll talk
in detail about each of the five stages through
which that happens—and the subtle ways
we can practice awareness more and more
kindfully in each stage. Meeting the beautiful
breath with a spirit of loving presence is a part

of practicing kindfulness that strengthens our ability to look after ourselves—and by kindfully looking after our own minds, we become more able to become a kindful force for good in the world.

Then, in the next part of this book, we'll turn our attention to kindful loving, the practice of opening wide the doors to our hearts. This practice also unfolds in five stages, and I'll offer guidance for each one, as we gradually generate kindfulness in our hearts and cultivate an ability to let it radiate, outward and unbounded, over the entire world. Kindful loving is a powerful way to care for others—and I'm certain you'll discover for yourself that through kindfully caring for others, your own life will become more and more wonderful, more and more beautiful.

Ajahn Brahm

Kindfulness

Don't Just Be Mindful, Be Kindful

A WEALTHY WOMAN went to her meditation class one evening. Many of her neighbors had been robbed, so she told the guard at the gate to her mansion to be alert and mindful at all times.

When she returned, she discovered that her mansion had been robbed. She scolded her guard, "I told you to be mindful of burglars. You have failed me."

"But I was mindful, ma'am," replied the guard. "I saw the burglars going into your mansion, and I noted, 'Burglar going in. Burglar going in.' Then I saw them coming out with all your jewelry, and I mindfully noted 'Jewelry going out. Jewelry going out.' Then I saw them going in again and taking out your safe, and I mindfully noted again, 'Safe being stolen. Safe being stolen.' I was mindful, ma'am."

Obviously, mindfulness is not enough!

Had the guard been kind to his employer as well as mindful, he would have called the police. When we add kindness to mindfulness we get "kindfulness."

A few years ago I had food poisoning. Monks of my tradition depend on almsfood, offered every day by our lay supporters. We never really know what we are eating, and we often put into our mouths something the stomach later has an argument with. An occasional stomachache is an occupational hazard for monks. But this time, it was far worse than a bout of indigestion. This was the agonizing cramps of food poisoning.

I took the opportunity to tap into the power of kindfulness.

I resisted the natural tendency to escape from the pain and felt the sensation as fully as I could. This is mindfulness—experiencing the feeling in the moment, as clearly as possible, without reacting. Then I added kindness. I opened the door of my heart to the pain, respecting it with emotional warmth. The mindfulness provided me with feedback. I noticed that my intestines had relaxed a little because of the kindness, and the pain was slightly less. So I continued with the kindfulness. Little by little, the pain decreased as the kindness did its job of relaxing the digestive tract. After only twenty minutes, the pain had gone, totally. I was as healthy and relaxed as if the food poisoning had never occurred.

Some may imagine there were other factors involved in my recovery but, personally, I know there weren't. I know the key ingredient was kindfulness. I took no medication, no water, no massage—it was the therapy of kindfulness, pure and simple. Of course, I had been training in this for over forty years—which may be why it was so effective. The cramps hurt like hell and made me double up in agony—but my suffering was countered by full-on kindfulness. I have no idea what happened to the bacteria that are the cause of food poisoning, but I didn't worry about that. The pain had gone completely. This is but one personal example of the power of kindfulness.

Kindfulness is the cause of relaxation.
It brings ease to the body,
to the mind, and to the world.
Kindfulness allows healing to happen.
Don't just be mindful, be kindful.

Kindfulness and Stillness

MANY PEOPLE TRY to practice meditation these days. Their biggest problem is that they cannot keep their mind still. No matter how hard they try, they are unable to stop thinking. Why? Let me tell you a story that may illuminate this.

A woman received a call one afternoon, "Hi, this is C.F. Are you free this afternoon for a cup of coffee?"

"Sure," the woman replied.

"Good," continued C.F. "We will go to that coffee shop that I like, not the one that you prefer. You will have a short black, not one of those high-cholesterol lattes that I know you like. You will have a blueberry muffin, just like me, not one of those silly pastries that I have seen you eat so often. We will sit in a quiet corner because that is where I want to sit, not out on the street where you always go. Then we will discuss politics, which is what I like to talk about, not that spiritual mumbo jumbo that you always twitter on about. Lastly, we will stay for sixty minutes, not fifty minutes nor seventy minutes, just exactly one hour, because that is how long I want to stay."

"Umm..." replied the woman thinking quickly, "I just remembered that I have to see my dentist this afternoon. Sorry, C.F., I can't make it."

Would you like to go out for a cup of coffee with someone who tells you where to go, what to eat and drink, where to sit, and what to discuss? No way!

And in case you haven't figured it out yet, C.F. stands for Control Freak.

Compare this to someone meditating. "Mind, listen up! We are going to meditate now. You are going to watch the breath, which is what I want to do, not wander off wherever you want. You are going to place your awareness on the tip of the nose, which I like to do, not outside on the street. And you are going to sit there for exactly sixty minutes, not a minute more or less."

When you are the control freak who treats your mind like a slave, no wonder your mind always tries to escape from you. It will think of useless memories, plan something that will never happen, fantasize, or fall asleep—anything to get away from you. That is why you can't keep still!

**You are a control freak—
that is why you can't keep still!**

The same woman receives a call, "Hi! K.F. here. Would you like to come for a coffee this afternoon? Where would you like to go? What would you like to drink and eat? We'll sit where you like, talk about your favorite topics, and stay as long as you like."

"Actually, I have a dentist appointment this afternoon," replies the woman. "Heck! Never mind the dentist. I'm coming to have coffee with you." Then they have such a relaxed and enjoyable time together that they stay much longer than anyone expected. K.F. stands of course for Kindfulness Freak.

What if you meditated by treating your mind like a best friend?

Treating your mind like a best friend involves approaching it with warm, engaging attitude: "Hey buddy! Do you want to meditate now?

What do you want to watch? How do you want to sit? You tell me how long." When you treat your mind with kindfulness, your mind does not want to wander off anywhere. It likes your company. You hang out together, chilling out, for far longer than you ever expected.

Prioritizing Kindfulness

AT A FAMOUS BUSINESS school some years ago, a professor delivered an extraordinary lecture on social economics to his graduate class. Without explaining what he was doing, the professor carefully placed a glass jar on his desk. Then, in view of his students, he brought out a bag full of stones and placed them one by one in the jar, until no more would go in. He asked his students, "Is the jar full?"

"Yes," they replied.

The professor smiled. From beneath the desk, the professor produced a second bag, this one full of gravel. He then managed to shake the smaller stones into the spaces between the bigger stones in the jar. A second time, he asked the students, "Is the jar full?"

"No," they answered. They were on to him by now.

They were correct, of course, for the professor produced a bag of fine sand. He managed to coax much of the sand into the spaces between the stones and the gravel within the jar. Again he asked, "Is the jar full?"

"Probably not, Professor, knowing you," the students replied.

Smiling at their answer, the professor brought out a small jug of water, which he poured into the jar full of stones, gravel, and sand. When no more water would fit in the jar, he put down the jug and looked at his class.

"So, what does this teach you?" he asked his students.

"That no matter how busy your schedule,"

offered one of the students, "you can always fit something more in!" It was a famous business school, after all.

"No!" thundered the professor emphatically. "What it shows is that if you want to get the big stones in, you have to put them in first."

It was a lesson in priorities.

Please ensure that you schedule in the "precious stones" first, or you'll never get around to them, to fit them into your day.

What are the big stones in your "jar"? What is most important to fit into your life? Can you find space for the precious stone of kindfulness?

Cause and Effect

THROUGH MEDITATION and stillness, you acquire the deep data from which you derive insight into cause-and-effect relationships. Much of the Buddha's teaching is about understanding cause and effect, or where things come from and why they arise. As disciples of the Buddha, if there's a problem, we investigate it. We use our reason and experience to find out where the problem came from and where it leads. If we see that it leads to a negative or harmful state of body and mind, then we know that it is unwholesome and not connected with wisdom. Next, we investigate backward, to see the process by which that problem arose.

When you have enough kindfulness, peace, and wisdom, you see a whole series of causes and effects. You understand where anger, guilt, depression, and fear come from; you see how they grow inside of you.

**When you see these things clearly,
you're able to catch them early;
and because you know they are
unwholesome and unskillful,
you're able to do something
about them.**

Once a negative mental state has taken hold of your mind, you can't do much except stand back and allow it to pass. The most important thing is to make sure you're aware of it so that you can lessen the problem the next time it arises. This was the practice of one of my fellow monks in Thailand. He had a very difficult time in his first few years, but I admired him because he stood up to the defilements in his mind. Even though sometimes he had so much suffering that he thought he was going to go crazy and that he would have to leave, he stayed. The first time he was going through a really difficult period, he expected the problem to get worse and worse, but to his surprise and relief, it just petered out. It ended because he hadn't fed into it. He now had a direct experience of the impermanent nature of those states.

Importantly, he also realized that the dark state hadn't gone away forever. He understood it as a process: he saw how it arose and what kept it going. He saw that he didn't need to do anything to stop it; he just needed to avoid feeding the fire and allow it to burn out on its own. Because he developed this insight, the next time he had a dark state of mind, it was much easier to deal with. He remembered his previous experience and realized that this problem, too, would end by itself. He didn't make it more than it was, wasn't afraid of it, and didn't get upset by it. Consequently, he found it easier to endure, and because of his greater insight, the problem wasn't as intense and didn't last as long as before. And when it passed away again, his wisdom was further reinforced. Each time the problem arose, it was shorter and easier to bear, until eventually the problem disappeared altogether. That's a beautiful example of wisdom in practice—simple wisdom, but wisdom nonetheless.

Every time we're able to apply wisdom to reduce or overcome our problems, that's kindfulness at work.

Kindful Not Just to People

LET ME TELL YOU a story about a man I'll call Thomas. Thomas had spent many months meditating in our monastery in Australia before returning to his home in Germany to pursue further studies. He told me this story of how kindfulness had made him twenty euros when he really needed it.

On Thomas's first day on the campus of a German university, an ATM emitted a strange sound as he passed—"A type of gurgling sound," as he described it. He imagined that the university ATM was welcoming him to campus.

From that day on, Thomas repeatedly sent thoughts of kindness to his friend the ATM whenever he passed it: "May your bank notes never run out," "May your customers never hit you when they discover they have no funds," "May you never suffer a short circuit," and so on.

After many months, Thomas was sitting in the warm sun having his lunch within a few feet of his friend, the ATM, when he heard the familiar gurgling sound again. He turned around to see a twenty-euro note emerge from the machine!

He had been by the ATM for at least fifteen minutes and no one had come close to the machine, let alone tried to make a withdrawal. He went to the machine, took the note, and then waved it in the air to see if anyone claimed it. No one did. Thomas, the poor student, said "*Danke*" to his friendly ATM and pocketed the cash.

I repeatedly interrogated Thomas as to the

truth of that tale. He vehemently insisted it was true so many times that I now believe him.

So please practice kindfulness with ATMs—in fact, be kindful to everyone and everything—and who knows, one day they may be kind to you!

Be kindful to everyone and everything.

Kindful Attention

IN THIS SECTION, I'm going to introduce you in detail to the first part of kindfulness, present-moment awareness and breath meditation.

This kind of meditation unfolds in stages. You may wish to go briskly through the practices described in this little book, but be very careful if you do. If you pass too quickly through the initial steps of learning to meditate, you may find that the preparatory work has not been completed. It's like trying to build a house on a makeshift foundation—the structure goes up very quickly, but it may come down too soon! You would be wise to spend a lot of time making the groundwork and foundations solid. Then, if you decide to proceed to the higher stories of the House of the Buddha, they will be stable.

After you've spent enough time with the kindfulness practices in this book that these become stable, solid, and deeply a part of yourself, you may wish to explore the teachings of the *jhanas*. My book *Mindfulness, Bliss, and Beyond* is a great place to start that exploration. But there's no need to hurry—the practices of kindfulness in this book can be thoroughly transformative in themselves.

Kindfulness is good in the beginning, good in the middle, good in the end.

STAGE ONE

Come to the Present

WHEN I TEACH MEDITATION, I like to begin at the simple stage of giving up the baggage of past and future. You may think that this is an easy thing to do, but it is not. Abandoning the past means not thinking about your work, your family, your commitments, your responsibilities, your good or bad times in childhood, and so on. You abandon all past experiences by showing no interest in them at all.

During meditation you become someone who has no history. It becomes unimportant whether you are an old hand at meditation or just a beginner.

As a person of no-history, you do not think about where you live, where you were born, who your parents were, or what your upbringing was like. All of that history you renounce. In this way, if you are meditating with others, everyone becomes equal—just a meditator.

If we abandon all that history, we are equal and free. We free ourselves of some of the concerns, perceptions, and thoughts that limit us, that stop us from developing the peace born of letting go. Every part of our history is finally released, even the memory of what happened just a moment ago. Whatever has happened no longer interests us, and we let it go.

Mind Like a Padded Cell

I DESCRIBE MEDITATION as developing a mind like a padded cell. When any experience, perception, or thought hits the wall of this cell, it does not bounce back. It no longer reverberates in our mind. It just sinks into the padding and stops. The past does not echo in our consciousness. Some people think that if they contemplate the past, they can somehow learn from it and solve their problems. But when we gaze at the past we invariably look through a distorted lens. Whatever we think it was like, in truth it was not quite like that at all! This is why people argue about what happened even a few moments ago.

It is well known to police who investigate

traffic accidents that two different eyewitnesses, both completely honest, may give conflicting accounts of the same accident. When we see just how unreliable our memory is, we will not overvalue the past. We can bury it, just as we bury a person who has died. We bury the coffin or cremate the corpse, and it is done with. When we sit down to meditation, we do the same with our history.

**Do not linger on the past.
Do not keep carrying around coffins
full of dead moments. If you do,
you weigh yourself down with
heavy burdens that do not really
belong to you. When you let go
of the past, you will be free in the
present moment.**

As for the future—the anticipations, fears, plans, and expectations—let that go too. The Buddha once said, "Whatever you think the future will be, it will always be something different." This future is known by the wise as uncertain, unknown, and unpredictable. It is often useless to anticipate the future, and in meditation it is always a great waste of time. You cannot know the future. It can be so strange, so weird, so completely beyond what you would expect.

The Mind Is Wonderful and Strange

When you work with your mind, you find that it is so strange. The mind can do wonderful and unexpected things.

MEDITATORS WHO ARE having a difficult time achieving a peaceful state of mind sometimes start thinking, "Here we go again, another half-hour of frustration." But often something strange happens: although they are anticipating failure, they reach a very peaceful meditative state.

When you think during your meditation, "How many more minutes are there to go?

How much longer do I have to endure this?" that is just wandering off into the future. If you truly pay attention, you may see the pain disappear in a twinkling. You simply cannot anticipate when that is going to happen.

Why Can't Every Day Be Payday?

As you begin to practice meditation, you may think that none of your meditation sessions are any good. But in the next meditation session you might sit down and everything becomes so peaceful and easy. "Wow!" you think. "Now I can meditate!"

But then the next meditation is as awful as the first ones. What's going on here?

My first meditation teacher told me something that at the time sounded quite strange. He said, "There is no such thing as a bad meditation." He was right.

All those meditations that you call bad or frustrating are where you do the hard work for your "wages." It's like a person who on Monday works all day but gets no money at the end of the day. "What am I doing this for?" she thinks. She works all day Tuesday and still gets nothing. Another bad day. All day Wednesday and Thursday she works, and still nothing to show for it. Four bad days in a row. Then along comes Friday. She does exactly the same work as before, and at the end of the day the boss gives her her wages. Wow! Why can't every day be a payday?

Why can't every meditation be a payday? During the difficult meditations you build up your credit, the reason for your success. In the hard meditations you build up your strength, which creates the momentum for peace. Then when there is enough credit, the mind goes into a good meditation, and it is a payday. But you must remember that it was in the so-called bad meditations that most of the work was done.

**Hard meditations create
the momentum for peace.**

The Past and Future Are Burdens

WHEN YOU ANTICIPATE the future by thinking, "How many more minutes until the bell rings?" you torture yourself. So be very careful not to pick up the heavy burden of the future: "How many more minutes to go?" or "What should I do next?"

If you are caught up in stories about the future, you are not paying attention to what is happening now. You are asking for trouble.

In this stage of meditation keep your attention right in the present moment, to the point where you don't even know what day it is or what time it is. Morning? afternoon?—don't know! All you know is what moment it is right now. In this way, you arrive at this beautiful "monastery time," where you are just meditating in the moment. You're not aware of how many minutes have gone or how many remain. You cannot even remember what day it is.

Once as a young monk in Thailand, I had actually forgotten what year it was!

It is marvelous to live in the realm that is timeless, a realm so much more free than the time-driven world we usually inhabit.

In the timeless realm, you experience this moment—just as all wise beings have been experiencing this moment for thousands of years. You have arrived at the reality of now.

When you have abandoned all past and all future, it is as if you have come alive. You are here. You are mindful. This is the first stage of meditation, just this mindfulness sustained only in the present. Practicing even this stage, you have done a great deal. You have let go of the first burden that stops deep meditation. So it is important to put forth a lot of effort to make this first stage strong, firm, and well established.

**The reality of now
is magnificent and awesome.**

Present-Moment Awareness

LETTING GO OF the first burden that stops deep meditation, obsession with past and future, now you can proceed to the even more beautiful and truthful silence of the mind.

As we begin to explore present-moment awareness, it is helpful to clarify the difference between experiencing the silent awareness of the present moment and merely *thinking* about it.

Let me offer a simile: Imagine watching a tennis match on TV. You may notice that two matches are occurring simultaneously: the match that you see on the screen and the match that you hear being described by the commentator. And the commentary is often biased. If an Australian is playing an American, for example, an Australian sportscaster is likely to provide a very different commentary from an American one. In this simile, watching the TV screen with no commentary stands for silent awareness in meditation, and paying attention to the commentary stands for thinking about it.

**You are much closer to truth
when you observe without commentary,
when you experience just
the silent awareness
of the present moment.**

Silent Awareness
in the Present Moment

**It is the inner speech that spins the
delusions that cause suffering.**

SOMETIMES WE ASSUME it is through
the inner commentary that we know the world.
Actually, that inner speech does not know the
world at all.

Inner speech causes us to be angry with our
enemies and to form dangerous attachments to
our loved ones. Inner speech causes all of life's
problems. It constructs fear and guilt, anxi-
ety and depression. It builds these illusions

as deftly as the skillful actor manipulates the audience to create terror or tears.

It is the high value that one gives to one's own thoughts that is the main obstacle to silent awareness. Wisely removing the importance that one gives to thinking, and realizing the greater accuracy of silent awareness, opens the door to inner silence.

If you seek truth, you should value silent awareness and, when meditating, consider it more important than any thought.

The Mind Hosts a Party

AN EFFECTIVE WAY to overcome the inner commentary is to develop a refined present-moment awareness. You watch every moment so closely that you simply don't have the time to comment about what has just happened. A thought is often an opinion on what has just happened: "That was good." "That was horrible." Or even, "What was that?" All of these comments are about the previous experience. When you are noting or making a comment about an experience that has just passed, you are not paying attention to the experience that has just arrived. You are dealing with old visitors and neglecting the new arrivals.

To develop this metaphor, imagine your mind to be a host at a party, meeting the guests as they come in the door. If one guest comes in and you start talking with this person about this or that, then you are not doing your duty of paying attention to each guest who enters. Since a guest comes in the door every moment, you must greet each one and then immediately greet the next. You cannot afford to engage even in the shortest conversation with any guest, since this would mean missing the one coming in next. In meditation, experiences come one by one through the doors of our senses into the mind.

If you greet one experience with mindfulness but then start a conversation with it, you will miss the next experience following right behind.

When you are perfectly in the moment with every experience, with every guest that comes into your mind, then you simply do not have the space for inner speech. You cannot chatter to yourself because you are completely taken up with mindfully greeting everything just as it arrives. This is refining present-moment awareness to the level that it becomes silent awareness of the present in every moment.

Set Down Your Backpack

IN DEVELOPING INNER silence you are giving up another great burden. It is as if you have been carrying a heavy rucksack on your back for thirty or fifty years continuously, and during that time you have wearily trudged for many, many miles. Now you have had the courage and found the wisdom to take that rucksack off and put it on the ground for a while. You feel so immensely relieved, so light, and so free, now that you are unburdened.

The Space Between Thoughts

ANOTHER USEFUL TECHNIQUE for developing inner silence is recognizing the space between thoughts, or between periods of inner chatter. Attend closely with sharp mindfulness when one thought ends and before another thought begins—there! That is silent awareness! It may be only momentary at first, but as you recognize that fleeting silence you become accustomed to it. And as you become accustomed to it, the silence lasts longer. You begin to enjoy the silence, once you have found it at last, and that is why it grows.

**Remember: silence is shy.
If silence hears you talking about
her, she vanishes immediately!**

Silence Is Delightful

IT WOULD BE MARVELOUS for each one of us if we could abandon all inner speech and abide in silent awareness of the present moment long enough to realize how delightful it is.

When one realizes how valuable silence is, silence becomes more attractive and important. The mind inclines toward it, seeks it out constantly, to the point where it engages in the thinking process only if it is really necessary, only if there is some point to it. Once we have realized that most of our thinking is really pointless, that it gets us nowhere and only gives us headaches, we gladly and easily spend much time in inner quiet. This second stage of the meditation, then, is silent present-moment awareness. We may want to spend much time developing just these first two stages, because if we can reach this point, we have come a long way indeed in our meditation. In that silent awareness of "just now," we experience much peace, joy, and consequent wisdom.

**Silence is so much more
productive of wisdom
and clarity
than thinking.**

Silent Present-Moment Awareness
of the Breath

IF WE WANT TO GO further, then instead
of being silently aware of whatever comes into
the mind, we choose silent present-moment
awareness of just one thing. I suggest you start
with silent present-moment awareness of the
breath.

**If we really pay attention,
we will discover that multiplicity of
consciousness is another heavy burden.**

Choosing to fix one's attention on one thing
is letting go of mental diversity and moving to
its opposite, unity. As the mind begins to unify

and sustain attention on just one thing, the experience of peace, bliss, and power increases significantly.

Such a consciousness is like having six telephones on your desk ringing at the same time. Letting go of this diversity and permitting only one telephone (a private line at that) on your desk is such a relief that it generates bliss. The understanding that diversity of mind is a heavy burden is crucial to being able to focus on the breath.

Careful Patience
Is the Fastest Way

It often happens that meditators start breath meditation when their minds are still jumping around between past and future, and when awareness is being drowned out by inner commentary. Without proper preparation they find breath meditation difficult, even impossible, and give up in frustration. They give up because they did not start at the right place. They did not perform the preparatory work before taking up the breath as a focus of their attention. However, if your mind has been well prepared by completing these first two stages, then when you turn to the breath you will be able to sustain your attention on it with ease.

If you find it difficult to attend to your breath, this is a sign that you rushed the first two stages. Go back to the preliminary exercises.

**Careful patience
is the fastest way!**

Don't Overcomplicate Things

WHEN YOU FOCUS on the breath, you focus on the experience of the breath happening now. You experience what the breath is doing, whether it is going in, going out, or is in between. Some teachers say to watch the breath at the tip of the nose, some say to watch it at the abdomen, and some say to move it here and then move it there.

I have found through experience that it does not matter where you watch the breath.

In fact it is best not to locate the breath anywhere. If you locate the breath at the tip of your nose then it becomes "nose aware-ness," not breath awareness, and if you locate it at your abdomen then it becomes "abdo-men awareness." Just ask yourself right now: "Am I breathing in or breathing out? How do I know?" There! The experience that tells you what the breath is doing, that is what you focus on. Let go of the concern about where this experience is located.

Just focus on the experience itself.

The Tendency
to Control Breathing

A COMMON PROBLEM at this stage is the tendency to control the breathing, and this makes the breathing uncomfortable. To overcome this difficulty, imagine that you are just a passenger in a car looking through the window at your breath. You are not the driver, nor a backseat driver.

Stop giving orders, let go, and enjoy the ride. Let the breath do the breathing and simply watch.

When you know the breath is going in or going out for about one hundred breaths in a row, not missing one, then you have achieved what I call the third stage of this meditation, which involves sustained attention on the breath.

Kindfulness of the Breath

AT THIS STAGE, I encourage you to bring kindfulness to your breath meditation. Observe your breath with loving-kindness.

As you begin your practice, think something like "breath, the door of my heart is open to you no matter how you feel, no matter what you do."

You will soon be looking at your breathing with compassion, embracing it as it is instead of finding fault. By adding kindfulness to the process of awareness, you have no expectations, since the breath seems more than good enough. If you practice in this way, you soon feel this attractive warmth toward the breath that brings joy to every in-breath and out-breath.

STAGE FOUR

Full Sustained Attention on the Breath

THE FOURTH STAGE occurs when your attention expands to take in every single moment of the breath. You know the in-breath at the very first moment, when the first sensation of inbreathing arises. Then you observe as those sensations develop gradually through the whole course of one in-breath, not missing even a moment of the in-breath. When that in-breath finishes, you know that moment. You see in your mind that last movement of the in-breath. You then see the next moment as a pause between breaths, and then many more moments of pause until the out-breath begins. You see the first moment of outbreathing and each subsequent sensation as the out-breath evolves, until the out-breath disappears when its function is complete. All this is done in silence and in the present moment.

You experience every part of each in-breath and out-breath continuously for many hundred breaths in a row. That is why this stage is called full sustained attention on the breath.

You cannot reach this stage through force, through holding, or through gripping.

You can attain this degree of stillness only by letting go of everything in the entire universe except for this momentary experience of the breath happening silently.

Actually "you" do not reach this stage at all, the mind does.

The mind does the work itself. The mind

recognizes this stage to be a very peaceful and pleasant place to abide, just being alone with the breath. This is where the doer, the major part of one's ego, starts to disappear.

One finds that progress happens effortlessly at this stage of meditation. We just have to get out of the way, let go, and watch it all happen.

The mind will automatically incline, if we only let it, toward this very simple, peaceful, and delicious unity of being alone with one thing, just being with the breath in each and every moment.

This is the unity of mind, the unity in the moment, the unity in stillness.

The Beginning of
the Beautiful Breath

THE FOURTH STAGE is what I call the "springboard" of meditation, because from it one may dive into the blissful states. When we simply maintain this unity of consciousness by not interfering, the breath will begin to disappear. The breath appears to fade away as the mind focuses instead on what is at the center of the experience of breath, which is awesome peace, freedom, and bliss.

At this stage I introduce the term "beautiful breath." Here the mind recognizes that this peaceful breath is extraordinarily beautiful. We are aware of this beautiful breath continuously, moment after moment, with no break in the chain of experience. We are aware only of the beautiful breath, without effort and for a very long time.

I have described the first four stages of meditation. Each stage must be well developed before going on to the next.

Please take a lot of time with these four initial stages, making them all firm and stable before proceeding.

You should be able to maintain with ease the fourth stage, full sustained attention on the breath, during every moment of the breath without a single break for two or three hundred breaths in succession. I am not saying you should count the breaths during this stage; I am just giving an indication of the approximate span of time that one should be able to stay in stage four before proceeding further.

It bears repeating: in meditation, careful patience is the fastest way!

Full Sustained Attention on the Beautiful Breath

THE FIFTH STAGE is called full sustained attention on the beautiful breath. Often this stage flows naturally and seamlessly from the previous stage. As briefly discussed in the previous chapter, when one's full attention rests easily and continuously on the experience of breathing with nothing interrupting the even flow of awareness, the breath calms down. It changes from a coarse, ordinary breath to a very smooth and peaceful "beautiful breath." The mind recognizes this beautiful breath and delights in it. It experiences a deepening of contentment. It is happy just to be watching this beautiful breath, and it does not need to be forced.

**If you try to *do something* at this stage,
you will disturb the whole process.**

"You" do not do anything. If you do something, the beauty will be lost. It's like landing on a snake's head in the game of snakes and ladders—you must go back many squares. From this stage of meditation on, the doer has to disappear. You are just a knower, passively observing.

Sometimes, though, you might give your mind the gentlest, most kindful of little nudges.

A helpful trick at this stage is to break the inner silence for a moment and gently say to yourself: "calm." That's all. At this stage of the meditation, the mind is usually so sensitive that just a little nudge causes it to follow the instruction obediently. The breath calms down and the beautiful breath emerges.

Beyond "In" and "Out"

WHEN WE ARE passively observing the beautiful breath in the moment, the perception of "in" (breath) or "out" (breath), or the beginning, middle, or end of a breath, should be allowed to disappear. All that remains will be the experience of the beautiful breath happening now. The mind is not concerned with what part of its cycle the breath is in or where in the body it occurs. Here we are simplifying the object of meditation. We are experiencing breath in the moment, stripped of all unnecessary details. We are moving beyond the duality of "in" and "out" and are just aware of a beautiful breath that appears smooth and continuous, hardly changing at all.

Do absolutely nothing and see how smooth, beautiful, and timeless the breath can be. See how calm you can allow the breath to be.

Take time to savor the sweetness of the beautiful, kindful breath— ever calmer, ever sweeter.

A Grin without a Cat

SOON THE BREATH will disappear, not when you want it to but when there is enough calm, leaving only the sign of "the beautiful."

In Lewis Carroll's *Alice in Wonderland*, Alice is startled to see the Cheshire Cat sitting on a bough of a nearby tree and grinning from ear to ear. Like all the strange creatures in Wonderland, the Cheshire Cat has the eloquence of a politician. Not only does the cat get the better of Alice in the ensuing conversation, but it also suddenly disappears and then, without warning, just as suddenly reappears.

Alice said, "...and I wish you wouldn't keep appearing and vanishing so suddenly: you make one quite giddy!"

"All right," said the Cat; and this time it vanished quite slowly, beginning with the end of the tail, and ending with the grin, which remained some time after the rest of it had gone.

"Well! I've often seen a cat without a grin," thought Alice; "but a grin without a cat! It's the most curious thing I ever saw in all my life!"

This story is an eerily accurate analogy for the meditation experience.

Just as the Cheshire Cat disappeared, leaving only its grin, so the meditator's body and breath disappear, leaving only "the beautiful." For Alice, it was the most curious thing she ever saw. For the meditator it is also strange, to clearly experience a free-floating beauty with nothing to embody it—not even a breath.

*Kindful Loving
and Letting Be*

Opening the Door of Your Heart

THE BUDDHA'S WORD for loving-kindness is *metta*, and this is an important component of kindfulness. It refers to an emotion, to that feeling of goodwill that can sustain thoughts wishing happiness for another, and that is willing to forgive any fault. My favorite expression of metta is encompassed by the words "the door of my heart is fully open to you, forever, whoever you are and whatever you have done."

Metta is love without a self, arising from inspiration, expecting nothing back in return, and without any conditions.

A Warm Fire in Your Heart

METTA CAN ACCURATELY be compared with a warm and radiant fire burning in your heart. You cannot expect to light the fire of loving-kindness by starting with a difficult object, any more than you can expect to light a campfire by striking a match under a thick log. So do not begin metta meditation by trying to spread metta to yourself or to an enemy. Instead begin by spreading loving-kindness to something that is easy to ignite with loving-kindness.

In metta meditation you focus your attention on the feeling of loving-kindness, developing that delightful emotion until it fills the whole mind. The way this is achieved can be compared to the way you light a campfire. You start with paper or anything else that is easy to light. Then you add kindling, small twigs, or strips of wood. When the kindling is on fire you add thicker pieces of wood, and after a time the thick logs. Once the fire is roaring and very hot, you can even put on wet and sappy logs and they are soon alight.

Kindfulness enables you to embrace other beings—as well as yourself— just as they and you are. Most people find this impossible because of their faultfinding mind.

Start with What's Easy to Love

I PREPARE MYSELF for metta meditation by imagining a little kitten. I like cats, especially kittens, so my imaginary kitten is to loving-kindness as gas is to a flame. I only need to think of my little kitten and my heart lights up with metta.

I continue to visualize my imaginary friend, picturing it as abandoned, hungry, and very afraid. In its short span of life it has only known rejection, violence, and loneliness. I imagine its bones sticking out from its emaciated body, its fur soiled with grime and some blood, and its body rigid with terror. I consider that if I don't care for this vulnerable little being then no one will, and it will die such a horrible, lonely, terrified death. I feel that kitten's pain fully, in all its forms, and my heart opens up, releasing a flood of compassion. I will care for that little kitten. I will protect it and feed it.

I imagine myself looking deeply into its anxious eyes, trying to melt its apprehension with the metta flowing through my own eyes. I reach out to it slowly, reassuringly, never losing eye contact. Gently, I pick up that little kitten and bring it to my chest. I remove the kitten's cold with the warmth from my own body, I take away its fear with the softness of my embrace, and I feel the kitten's trust grow. I speak to the kitten on my chest:

"Little being, never feel alone again.
Never feel so afraid. I will always look
after you, be your protector and friend.
I love you, little kitten. Wherever you go,

whatever you do, my heart will always welcome you. I give you my limitless loving-kindness always."

When I do this, I feel my kitten become warm, relax, and finally purr.

This is but an outline of how I begin my meditation on metta. I usually take much more time. I use my imagination and inner speech to paint a picture in my mind, to create a scenario where the first flames of metta can arise.

At the end of the mental exercise, my eyes still closed, I focus the attention on the region around my heart and feel the first warm glow of the emotion of kindfulness.

Find Your Own Kindling

MY KITTEN IS LIKE the paper that you use to start the campfire. You may not like kittens, so choose something else, a puppy or a baby perhaps. Whatever you choose as your first object of metta, make it an imaginary being and not a real one. In your mind you can make a kitten or a puppy or a baby into anything you like. You have more freedom to generate metta when you make use of a fantasy creature, rather than one from the real world.

My imaginary kitten purrs at all the right times— and never poops in my lap.

Having chosen your first object, use your powers of imagination to create a story around that being that arouses your loving-kindness. With practice this innovative method becomes one of the most successful and enjoyable ways to practice kindfulness.

Kindfulness-Block

SOME YEARS AGO a female student complained to me that this method did not work for her. She regarded small animals, especially mischievous kittens, as little pests, nor did she like crying-and-wailing nappy-soiling babies.

My student had a severe case of what I now call "kindfulness-block."

She went on to tell me that in her apartment in Sydney she had been growing some flowers in pots. So I suggested that she choose one of her plants as her first object of metta. She imagined a seedling so delicate and tender. It was so fragile that it needed all her care, love, and protection to survive. She directed all her motherly instincts to that vulnerable little potted plant, nurturing and feeding her friend until it burst from its bud to repay her kindness with a beautiful, fragrant flower. She really took to that method. That was the first time metta meditation worked for her. During the retreat when this happened, she said it was the only session when she wasn't waiting for me to ring the bell.

STAGE TWO

A Loved Person Close to You

AFTER THE FIRST FLAMES of metta have been established in this way, let go of your imaginary creature and put in its place a real person, someone very close to you emotionally such as your partner, a well-loved relation, or even your very best friend. It must be someone for whom it is easy to generate and sustain loving-kindness. In the metaphor of the campfire, they will be the thin pieces of wood called kindling. Once again use your inner speech to paint a picture around them in your mind. They too need your friendship and love. They are also emotionally vulnerable, subject to the disappointments and frustrations of life. Using your inner commentary say,

"Dearest friend, I sincerely wish
you happiness. May your body
be free from pain and your mind
find contentment. I give you my love
with no conditions. I'll always be
there for you. You will always
have a place in my heart.
I truly care for you."

You can of course use similar words of your own design. Use whatever phrases arouse the warm glow of metta in your heart. Stay with this person. Imagine they are right before you until the metta grows bright and constant around them. Now briefly place your attention on your body near your heart and feel the physical sensation associated with metta.

You will find it feels delightful.

A Close Acquaintance, and a Group

LET GO OF THE IMAGE of that person and substitute that of another close acquaintance, creating the feeling of metta around them by using your inner speech in the same way: "May you live in happiness..." Imagine them right before you until the metta glows bright and constant around them.

Next substitute an entire group of people, perhaps all the people who live in your house. Develop the caring glow of metta around them in the same way: "May you be well and happy..." In the simile of the campfire, you are now putting on the logs.

Golden Radiance

SEE IF YOU CAN IMAGINE metta to be a golden radiance emanating from a beautiful white lotus flower in the middle of your heart. Allow that radiance of loving-kindness to expand in all directions, embracing more and more living beings until it becomes boundless, filling up all that you can imagine. "May all living beings, near or far, great or small, be happy and at peace..."

Bathe the whole universe in the warmth of the golden light of kindfulness. Stay there for a while.

In the simile of the campfire, the fire is now roaring and very hot and can now burn the wet and sappy logs. Think about your enemy. Visualize someone who has hurt you badly. You will be astonished that your metta is now strong enough for you to forgive them. You are now able to share the healing golden glow of loving-kindness with them as well: "Friend, whatever you have done to me, revenge will not help either of us, so instead I wish you well. I sincerely wish you freedom from the pain of the past and joy in all your future. May the beauty of this unconditional loving-kindness reach you as well, bringing you happiness and contentment." When the fire of metta burns strong, nothing can withstand it. Next, there is one final "wet and sappy stick" to be tossed into the fire of metta. Most meditators find that the hardest person to give loving-kindness to... is themselves.

STAGE FIVE

Include Yourself

IMAGINE THAT YOU are looking at yourself in a mirror. Say this with your inner speech and with total sincerity: "I wish myself well. I now give myself the gift of happiness. Too long the door of my heart has been closed to me; now I open it. No matter what I have done, or will ever do, the door to my own love and respect is always open to me. I forgive myself unreservedly. Come home. I now give myself the love that does not judge. I care for this vulnerable being called 'me.' I embrace all of me with the loving-kindness of metta." Invent your own words here to let the warmth of loving-kindness sink deep inside of you, to the part that is most frightened. Let it melt all resistance until you are at one with metta, unlimited loving-kindness, like a mother's care for her child.

Ending the Meditation

BEFORE YOU END the metta meditation, pause for a minute or two and reflect on how you feel inside. Notice the effect that this meditation has had on you. Metta meditation can produce truly wonderful experiences.

To bring the meditation to an elegant conclusion, once more imagine metta as a golden glow radiating from the beautiful white lotus located in your heart.

Visualize the golden radiance of kindfulness being drawn back into the lotus, leaving the warmth outside.

When the golden glow becomes like a condensed ball of incandescent energy in the center of the white lotus, imagine the petals closing around the ball of metta, guarding the seed of loving-kindness within your heart, ready to be released again in your next metta meditation. Open your eyes and get up slowly.

Letting Be:
Another Form of Kindfulness

SOMETIMES INSTEAD OF TAKING
loving-kindness or the breath as my object in
meditation, I look at my mind and realize the
best thing it needs at the moment is just to
let things be. Basically, letting-be meditation
is a variety of silent awareness of the present
moment. It has to be silent, because to really
let things be means you give no orders and
have no complaints; you've got nothing to talk
about.

**Letting be happens
in the present moment.**

You're aware of things as they appear right now, and you allow them to come in or stay or go, whenever they want. Letting-be meditation is like sitting in a room, and whoever comes in the door, you let in. They can stay as long as they like. Even if they are terrible demons, you allow them to come in and sit down. You are not at all fazed. If the Buddha himself enters in all his glory, you just sit here just the same, completely equanimous. "Come in if you want." "You can go whenever." Whatever comes into your mind, the beautiful or the horrible, you stand back and let it be, with no reactions at all—quietly observing and practicing silent awareness in the present moment. This is letting-be meditation.

Don't try to make everything perfect or tie up all those loose ends before you let things be. Life is never perfect and duties are never finished.

Kindful letting be is having
the courage to sit quietly
and rest the mind
in the midst of imperfection.

If All Else Fails…

LETTING-BE MEDITATION can become quite powerful. If your breath meditation or metta meditation or any other type of meditation isn't working, very often it's because the foundation is incorrect. So just do the letting-be meditation. Whatever is happening, that's OK. Whatever you're experiencing is fine—no preference, no choice, no good or bad, no argument, and no commentary. Just let things be. You can have a little bit of inner speech, but only a commentary about "letting be."

Just be with what is.
This too is kindfulness.

Just be with thoughts concerned with the meditation subject, but not about anything else. That way the meditation comes close to complete silent awareness of the present moment.

If I'm in pain, if I have a headache, stomach-ache, or some other ache, or if the mosquitoes are biting, I say, "Just let it be." I don't argue with it, don't get upset about it. I just watch the feelings in my body as the mosquito pushes its nose into my flesh and itching sensations follow. "Just let things be." If you're lying in bed at night and you can't go to sleep: "Let it be." Or if there's a pain that won't go away: "Just let it be." Just be with it. Don't try running away. If demons have come into your room, you're not going to push them out, but you're not going to invite them to stay either. You're just going to let them be.

Letting be is the practice of equanimous kindfulness.

This Is Good Enough

MY OWN ABILITY in meditation comes from my attitude of saying, "This is good enough," to whatever I'm experiencing. Ability in meditation is all about attitude: as long as I can watch the breath, that's good enough for me. So when you meditate, be contented and easily satisfied.

This is not being lazy, but part of the true practice of kindfulness.

Working with Obstacles to Kindfulness

IT'S EASY TO FIND reasons to not practice kindfulness. All kinds of obstacles arise. In this section, I'll offer some suggestions on skillfully working with a variety of the most common of such obstacles and some tools to help you do so.

Not Disturbing Disturbances

FOR EXAMPLE, when we are meditating and hear a sound, why can't we simply ignore it? Why does it disturb us so? Many years ago in Thailand the local villages surrounding our monastery held a party. The noise from the loudspeakers was so loud that it seemed to destroy the peace in our monastery. So we complained to our teacher, Ajahn Chah, that the noise was disturbing our meditation. The great master replied, "It is not the noise that disturbs you, it is you who disturb the noise!" Similarly, when your meditation is interrupted by a pain in your legs, for instance, then it is not the pain that disturbs you but it is you who disturb the pain.

Making Peace with Sloth and Torpor

**Make peace not war
with sloth and torpor.**

THE MOST PROFOUND and effective way of overcoming sloth and torpor is to make peace with the dullness and stop fighting it! When I was a young monk in the forest monasteries in Thailand and became sleepy during the 3:15 a.m. sitting, I would struggle like hell to overpower the dullness. I would usually fail. But when I did succeed in overcoming my sleepiness, restlessness would replace it. So I would calm down the restlessness and fall back into sloth and torpor. My meditation was like a pendulum swinging between extremes and never finding the middle. It took many years to understand what was going on.

The Buddha advocated investigation, not fighting.

So I examined where my sloth and torpor came from. I had been meditating at 3:15 in the morning, having slept very little, I was malnourished, an English monk in a hot tropical jungle—what would you expect! The dullness was the effect of natural causes. I let go and made peace with my sleepiness. I stopped fighting and let my head droop. Who knows, I might even have snored. When I stopped fighting sloth and torpor it did not last all that long. Moreover, when it passed I was left with peace and not with restlessness. I had found the middle of my pendulum swing and I could observe my breath easily from then on.

Dullness in meditation is the result of a tired mind, usually one that has been overworking. Fighting that dullness makes you even more exhausted. Resting allows the energy to return to the mind. The most profound and effective way to overcome sloth and torpor is to stop fighting your mind.

Stop trying to change things and instead let things be.

Remorse about the Past

Everyone makes mistakes.

REMORSE IS THE RESULT of hurtful things that you may have done or said. In other words, it is a result of bad conduct. If any remorse comes up in meditation, instead of dwelling on it, you should forgive yourself. The wise are not people who never make mistakes, but those who forgive themselves and learn from their mistakes. Some people have so much remorse that they think they can never become enlightened.

Restlessness and Contentment

RESTLESSNESS ARISES because we do not appreciate the beauty of contentment. We do not acknowledge the sheer pleasure of doing nothing. We have a faultfinding mind rather than a mind that appreciates what's already there. Restlessness in meditation is always a sign of not finding joy in what's here. Whether we find joy or not depends on the way we train our perception. It's within our power to change the way we look at things. We can look at a glass of water and perceive it as very beautiful, or we can think of it as ordinary. In meditation, we can see the breath as dull and routine, or we can see it as very beautiful and unique. If we look upon the breath as something of great value, then we won't get restless. We won't go around looking for something else. That's what restlessness is, going around looking for something else to do, something else to think about, somewhere else to go—anywhere but here and now. Restlessness is one of the major hindrances, along with sensory desire. Restlessness makes it so hard to sit still for very long.

Contentment is the opposite of a faultfinding mind.

You should develop the perception of contentment with whatever you have, wherever you are, as much as you can—and beware of finding fault in your meditation.

Watch the silence and be content to be silent. If you're truly content, you don't need to say anything. Don't most inner conversations take the form of complaining, attempting to change things, or wanting to do something else? Or escaping into the world of thoughts and ideas? Thinking indicates a lack of contentment. If you're truly contented, then you're still and quiet. See if you can deepen your contentment, because it is the antidote for restlessness.

Even if you have an ache in the body and don't feel well, you can change your perception and regard that as something quite fascinating, even beautiful. See if you can be content with the ache or pain. See if you can allow it to be. A few times during my life as a monk I have been in quite severe pain. Instead of trying to escape, which is restlessness, I turned my mind around to completely accept the pain and be content with it. I have found that it is possible to be content with even severe pain. If you can do that, the worst part of the pain disappears along with the restlessness. There's no wanting to get rid of it. You're completely still with the feeling. The restlessness that accompanies pain is probably the worst part. Get rid of restlessness through contentment, and you can even have fun with pain.

Develop contentment with whatever you have—the present moment, the silence, the breath. So if you ever see restlessness in your mind, remember the word *contentment*.

Wherever you are, develop contentment, and from that contentment— out of the very center of that contentment— you'll find your kindfulness will deepen.

Many Kinds of Doubt

THERE ARE MANY KINDS of doubts that can become obstacles to practicing kindfulness. Doubt can be toward the teaching, about the teacher, or toward yourself.

Regarding doubt toward the teaching, if you really pay honest attention, you can see that even in your own experience some beautiful results come from practicing meditation. With regard to teachers, they are often like coaches of sports teams. Their job is to teach from their own experience and, more important, to inspire students with words and deeds. But before you put your confidence in a teacher, check them out. Observe their behavior and see for yourself if they are practicing what they preach. If they really know what they are talking about, then they will be ethical, restrained, and inspiring. Only if teachers lead by example—a good example, that is—should you place your confidence in them.

Doubt can also be directed toward what you are experiencing now: "What is this? Is this the beautiful breath? Is this present-moment awareness?" Engaging such thoughts is inappropriate during meditation. Just make the mind as peaceful as you can. Let go and enjoy the peace and happiness. Afterward, if you like, you can review the meditation and ask, "What was that? That was really interesting. What was happening there?"

Self-doubt is one of the most pernicious forms of doubt. Self-doubt thinks, "I'm hopeless, I can't do this, I'm useless, I'm sure everyone else who practices meditation, except me, is having an easy time of it." This is often overcome with the help of a teacher who inspires and encourages you. Seeking out a good teacher is enormously worthwhile. Have confidence that you can achieve whatever you want.

If you have sufficient determination and confidence, then it's only a matter of time before you succeed. The only people who fail are those who give up.

Ill Will

Ill will toward yourself may be the main reason why your meditation is difficult.

MANY PEOPLE FIND IT particularly diffi-cut to be kindful to themselves. Ill will toward yourself can manifest as not allowing your-self to peacefully settle into meditation, or to become successful in meditation.

I suggest this simple solution: Give yourself a break. Say to yourself, "The door to my heart is open to all of me. I allow myself happiness. I allow myself peace. I have goodwill toward myself, enough goodwill to let myself become peaceful and to bliss out on this meditation."

If you find it hard to extend loving-kindness toward yourself, ask why. There may be a deep-seated guilt complex inside, and you still expect punishment. You haven't given yourself unconditional forgiveness.

On the other hand, ill will toward the meditation object is a common problem for people who have been meditating on the breath without much success yet. I say "yet" because it's only a matter of time. Everyone will have success if they follow the instructions. But if you haven't succeeded yet, you may have some ill will toward meditation or the meditation object. You may sit down and think, "Oh, here we go again," "This is going to be difficult," "I don't really want to do this," "I have to do this because it's what meditators do," or "I've got to be a good Buddhist, and this is what Buddhists are supposed to do."

If you start the meditation with ill will toward meditation, doing it but not liking it, then it's not going to work.

You are putting a hindrance in front of yourself straightaway. Try treating meditation as a dear old friend, one you want to spend time with. You're willing to drop everything else. If I see a meditation a mile away I just run toward it and give it a good old hug and take it for a cup of coffee somewhere. And as for the meditation object, the breath, we've had such good times together, my breath and I. We're the best of mates. If you regard the breath with that sort of goodwill, you can see why it's so easy to watch the breath in your meditation.

To sum up, ill will is a hindrance, and you overcome that hindrance by compassion to all others, forgiveness toward yourself, loving-kindness toward the meditation object, goodwill toward the meditation, and friendship toward the breath. You can have loving-kindness toward silence and the present moment too. When you care for these friends who reside in the mind, you overcome any aversion toward them as meditation objects. When you have loving-kindness toward the meditation object, you do not need much effort to hold it. You just love it so much that it becomes effortless to be with.

One form that ill will can take is anger. In the next few sections of the book, we'll look a little more deeply at anger.

All the hindrances emanate from a single source: they are generated by the control freak inside of you that refuses to let things go.

Anger on Trial

IN ORDER TO EXPRESS your anger, you first have to justify it to yourself. You have to convince yourself that anger is deserved, appropriate, right. In the mental process that is anger, it is as if a trial occurs in your mind.

The accused stands waiting in the court in your mind. You are the prosecutor. You know they are guilty, but, to be fair, you have to prove it to the judge, your conscience, first. You launch into a graphic reconstruction of the "crime" committed against you.

You infer all sorts of malice, duplicity, and sheer cruelty of intention behind the accused's deed. You dredge up from the past their many other "crimes" against you to convince your conscience that they deserve no mercy.

In a real court of law, the accused has a lawyer too who is allowed to speak. But in this mental trial, you are in the process of justifying your anger. You, as judge, preemptively strike down all pathetic excuses or unbelievable explanations or weak pleas for forgiveness. The lawyer for the defense is not allowed to speak. In your one-sided argument, you construct a convincing case. That's good enough. Your conscience brings down the hammer and the accused is found guilty! Now we feel okay at being angry with them.

Many years ago, this is the process I saw happen in my own mind whenever I got angry. It seemed so unfair. So the next time I wanted to get angry with someone, I paused to let "the counsel for defense" have a say. Serving this role, I thought up plausible excuses and probable explanations for the accused's behavior. I eloquently testified to the importance and beauty of forgiveness. And then I found that the mental court of my informed conscience would no longer allow a verdict of guilty. And thus it became impossible to pass judgment on the behavior of another. Anger, not being justifiable, was deprived of its fuel and died.

The Anger-Eating Demon

A problem with anger is that we enjoy being angry.

THERE IS AN ADDICTIVE and powerful pleasure associated with the expression of anger. And we don't want to let go of what we enjoy. However, there is also a danger in anger, a consequence that outweighs any pleasure. If we would keep in mind the danger, then we would be willing to let anger go.

In a palace, in a realm a long time ago, a demon walked in while the king was away. The demon was so ugly, he smelled so bad, and what he said was so disgusting, that the guards and other palace workers froze in horror. This allowed the demon to stride right through the outer rooms, into the royal audience hall, and then sit himself on the king's throne. Seeing the demon on the king's throne, the guards and the others came to their senses.

"Get out of here!" they shouted. "You don't belong there! If you don't move your butt right now, we'll carve it out with our swords!"

At these few angry words, the demon grew a few inches bigger, his face grew uglier, the smell got worse, and his language became even more obscene.

Swords were brandished, daggers pulled out, threats made. At every angry word or angry deed, even at every angry thought, that demon grew an inch bigger, more ugly in appearance, more smelly, and more foul in his language.

This confrontation had been going on for quite a while when the king returned. He saw on his own throne this gigantic demon. He had never seen anything so repulsively ugly before, not even in the movies. The stench coming from the demon would even make a maggot sick. And his language was more repugnant than anything you'd hear in the roughest of drunk-filled downtown bars on a Saturday night.

The king was wise. That's why he was king: he knew what to do.

"Welcome," he said warmly. "Welcome to my palace. Has anyone gotten you anything to drink yet? or to eat?"

At those few kind gestures, the demon grew a few inches smaller, less ugly, less smelly, and less offensive.

The palace personnel caught on very quickly. One asked the demon if he would like a cup of tea. "We have Darjeeling, English Breakfast, or Earl Grey. Or do you prefer a nice peppermint? It's good for your health." Another phoned out for pizza, monster-size for such a big demon, while others made sandwiches (deviled-ham, of course). One soldier gave the demon a foot massage, while another massaged the scales on his neck. "Mmmm! That was nice," thought the demon.

At every kind word, deed, or thought, the demon of anger grows smaller, less ugly, less smelly, and less offensive.

Before the pizza boy arrived with his delivery, the demon had already shrunk to the size he was when he first sat on the throne. But they never stopped being kind. Soon the demon was so small that he could hardly be seen. Then after one more act of kindness he vanished completely away.

We call such monsters "anger-eating demons."

Many Kinds of
Anger-Eating Demons

YOUR PARTNER CAN SOMETIMES be an "anger-eating demon." Get angry with them and they get worse—more ugly, more smelly, and more offensive in their speech. The problem gets an inch bigger every time you are angry with them, even in thought. Perhaps you can see your mistake now and know what to do.

Pain is another "anger-eating demon." When we think with anger, Pain! Get out of here! You don't belong!, pain grows an inch bigger and worse in other ways. It is difficult to be kind to something so ugly and offensive as pain, but there will be times in our life when we have no other option. When we welcome pain, truly, sincerely, it becomes smaller, less of a problem, and sometimes vanishes completely.

Some cancers, for instance, are "anger-eating demons," ugly and repugnant monsters sitting in our body, our "throne." It is natural to say "Get out of here! You don't belong!" When all else fails, or maybe even earlier, perhaps we can say, "Welcome." Some feed on stress—that's why they are "anger-eating demons." Those kinds of cancers respond well when the "King of the Palace" courageously says: "Cancer, the door of my heart is fully open to you, whatever you do. Come in!"

If You Get Into Difficulty…

IF YOU GET INTO any difficulty in your meditation, stop and ask yourself, "Which of the hindrances is this?" Find out what the cause is. Once you know the cause, then you can remember the solution and apply it. If it's sensory desire, just take the attention away from the five senses little by little and apply it to the breath or the mind. If it's ill will, do some loving-kindness. For sloth and torpor, remember "give value to awareness." If it's restlessness and remorse, remember "contentment, contentment, contentment" or practice forgiveness. And if it's doubt, be confident and be inspired by the teachings. Whenever you meditate, apply the solutions methodically. That way, the obstacles you experience won't create long-term barriers.

Every obstacle is ultimately something that you can recognize, overcome, and move beyond.

When Your Mind's Like a Raging Elephant

Some meditators experience all the hindrances at once—and in great force.

AT THE TIME they think they might go crazy. To help such meditators with their acute and intense attack of all hindrances, I teach the Nalagiri Strategy based on a well-known episode from the life of the Buddha.

Enemies tried to kill the Buddha by releasing an intoxicated bull elephant named Nalagiri in the narrow street where the Buddha was walking for alms. Those who saw the mad elephant charging shouted warnings to the Buddha and his following of monks to quickly get out of the way. All the monks fled except for the Buddha and his faithful attendant, Venerable Ananda. Ananda bravely moved in front of his master, ready to protect his beloved teacher by sacrificing his own life. Gently the Buddha pushed Ananda to the side and faced the immensely powerful charging elephant alone. The Buddha certainly possessed psychic powers, and I believe he could have grabbed the great elephant by the trunk, twirled him three times in the air above his head, and thrown him over the river Ganges hundreds of miles away! But that is not the way of a Buddha. Instead he used loving-kindness and the power of letting go. Perhaps the Buddha thought something like "Dear Nalagiri, the door of my heart is open to you no matter what you ever do to me. You may swat me with your trunk or crush me under your feet, but I will give you no ill will. I will love you unconditionally." The Buddha gently placed peace in the space between him and the dangerous elephant. Such is the irresistible power of authentic kindfulness and letting go that in a few seconds the elephant's rage had subsided, and Nalagiri was meekly bowing before the Compassionate One, having his trunk gently stroked "There, there, Nalagiri, there, there..."

There are times in some meditators' practice when their mind is as crazy as an intoxicated bull elephant charging around smashing everything. In such situations please remember the Nalagiri Strategy.

Don't use force to subdue your raging bull elephant of a mind.

When your mind is raging, use kindfulness and letting go: "Dear crazy mind of mine, the door of my heart is fully open to you no matter what you ever do to me. You may destroy or crush me, but I will give you no ill will. I love you, my mind, no matter what you ever do." Make peace with your crazy mind instead of fighting it. Such is the power of authentic loving-kindness and letting go that, in a surprisingly short time, the mind will be released from its rage and stand meekly before you as your soft kindfulness gently strokes it "There, there, mind; there, there..."

Arousing Energy

ONE FACTOR NEEDED for kindfulness is energy. You need energy at each stage, and that energy is aroused by putting everything you have into what you're doing. Don't keep anything back for the next moment. One of the mistakes that people make—especially with mental energy—is thinking, "If I put a lot of energy into this moment, I'll have nothing left for the next moment." It doesn't work that way with the mind. The more energy you put into this moment, the more you have for the next.

There is a limitless store of mental energy.

Recognizing and Avoiding the Snakes

We should use our understanding of these negative states of mind to inform our kindfulness.

WHEN WE'RE KINDFUL, we can start to see these mental and physical states growing, and because of our understanding, we can take remedial action before they get too entrenched.

During my early years in Thailand, there were lots of snakes in Wat Pah Pong. We often didn't have sandals because they fell apart so quickly, even though we did our best to tie them together with pieces of string or old strips of cotton cloth. At times we didn't even have flashlights—we would use them until they were really dead and couldn't generate even a flicker of light. Then we had to walk barefoot on those snake-infested paths with only the starlight to help us find our way. But because I knew there might be snakes on those paths, I set up my attention to look out for them and regard them as dangers to be avoided. Because of that, I never got bitten.

To avoid being bitten by negative states of mind, use kindfulness to stay aware of the dangers.

You know that negative mental states will not lead to peace but to more disturbances; they are bad habits that destroy happiness and lead to suffering. And like snakes, once they get you, you're in big trouble. So use your kindfulness to recognize these negative states as soon as they arise and then take another route—that is, use a strategy to avoid them. In this way you reduce your problems. Your wisdom is creating a more peaceful, happy, and healthy life, and you flow through the world with ease.

> **Although a happy and healthy life is its own reward, there are further, more profound benefits from overcoming negative mental states.**

Because negative states are suffering, people often react to them with further negativity, leading to feelings of anger, depression, or guilt. When you use kindfulness and wisdom to reduce or even resolve that suffering, you don't need to escape into fantasies or daydreams, and it's easier to retain a pure mind. This in turn makes you more joyful, and it becomes easier to get into stillness and strengthen your wisdom. You achieve a self-supporting cycle that gets more and more powerful as you go along.

And it's all because you're using your wisdom.

The Fault-Finding Mind

In the ancient Buddhist texts, you find that people found fault even with the Buddha!

WATCH OUT FOR NEGATIVITY, because it feeds the fault-finding mind. Fault-finding is an attitude that arises and then gets hold of you, just as a snake might, and it poisons your mind. Once the fault-finding is well established, there's no end to the things you can find fault with.

You may have the most perfect of monasteries, the most hard-working of teachers, the best food in the world, and the most comfortable hut, yet you can still find fault with all of it.

As a young monk I would sometimes find fault even with Ajahn Chah, and afterward I would feel really stupid. If I could find fault with him, the wisest and most selfless person I had ever met, then it was quite clear that the problem was with me, not with Ajahn Chah.

Once you get into fault-finding, you also end up applying it to yourself. On retreats, people often find fault with their practice: "I still haven't achieved anything; I've just been sleeping for the last few days."

Be careful:
fault-finding soon leads to guilt.
Guilt in turn leads to punishment,
and then kindfulness stalls—at best.

The AFL Code

The AFL Code:
Acknowledge, Forgive, Learn

WHEN WE PRACTICE KINDFULNESS, we commit to using the AFL code: Acknowledge, Forgive, and Learn. If we make a mistake, instead of beating ourselves up, we simply acknowledge it: "All right, I was late. I slept in this morning." Next we really forgive. There's no point to punishment—wisdom, real wisdom, knows that punishment just makes the problem worse by creating more unskillful states of mind.

When we forgive, we're letting go, and that leads to peace. Only if something leads to peace, freedom, and release is it a wise thing to do.

When you see that fault-finding is leading you in the wrong direction, you learn to avoid it altogether in the future.

It's much more productive to simply let go of the past or, even better, to recall that part of the past that was pleasant. You learn far more from your pleasant memories of past success and happiness than you ever learn from your suffering. When you remember what worked in the past, it encourages you, stops the fault-finding, and illuminates the causes of success. So drop all the lazy and restless meditations, and remember and learn from the good ones. Even if you only had one good meditation and you only watched the breath for five minutes, remember that! It encourages, informs, and leads you to greater peace. It's the way of wisdom.

Something to Be Avoided

WE SHOULD SEE THE fault-finding mind as a problem, a snake, a danger to be avoided. People sometimes write books with a fault-finding attitude in order to destroy authority, tradition, and institutions.

It's common in the West to think that fault-finding is good—but this is not so. Some years ago, someone visited Wat Pah Nanachat for three or four weeks and then wrote a book about his experiences. He really blasted the monastery and Ajahn Chah. He focused on everything that he thought was wrong, and consequently the book was completely unfair and unbalanced. People do this sort of thing because, as with anger, there's a certain pleasure in fault-finding. But be careful, because the danger far outweighs the pleasure. When you know this, you realize the fault-finding mind is a snake, and you can start to avoid it in the future.

In my experience, as much as 90 percent of any real practice of kindfulness is about understanding the fault-finding mind. This includes understanding where it comes from, how to avoid it, and how to develop the positive mind—how to see the nine hundred and ninety-eight good bricks, not just the two bad ones, in a wall you've constructed. Instead of fault-finding, try to understand human beings, yourself included, and have forgiveness and loving-kindness.

Practicing kindfulness means seeing yourself as just a person on the path, this poor little being who has suffered a lot already and who doesn't want more suffering. If you can be at peace with your suffering, you'll find that compulsive fault-finding decreases.

A Spotlight on Reality

As you build up kindfulness and it gets sharper, you will realize that you are emerging from a world that has been very dim. As you get more and more kindful, it's as if someone has turned on the lights in the room, or the sun has come out, illuminating the surroundings. You see so much more of what's around you. It's like shining a spotlight on reality, and you begin to see the subtle beauty of rich colors, delightful shapes, and deep textures. It all appears very beautiful and wonderful.

When you have developed powerful kindfulness, it's like going out into a beautiful garden in the brilliant sunshine. It's energizing and inspiring. Possessing strong kindfulness, such brightness of mind, if you then focus it on a small part of the world, then you will see so deeply into its nature. The experience of bright and focused awareness is wonderful and amazing! You see much more beauty and truth than you ever imagined.

Developing kindfulness is like turning up the lights of the mind.

When you sustain your attention on one thing instead of letting it wander all over the place, kindfulness builds up its own energy. You begin to see into things very deeply and wonderfully.

Going Forth Kindfully

The Path Is Not Hard to Follow

SINCE YOU HAVE A MIND, you also inevitably have thoughts. Walking the path of kindfulness doesn't necessarily mean having no thoughts, but rather having thoughts of renunciation, kindness, and gentleness toward all beings—including yourself. When your heart feels free, it's because you've practiced these three kinds of "right thought."

When you practice kindfulness, please remember what wisdom is. If something leads to well-being, tranquility, happiness, peace, and freedom, it must be a wisdom practice. But if negative qualities are created, then you're on the wrong track, and you're not practicing wisely. So investigate—find out what the wrong track is, and don't go there again; see it as a snake and avoid it. If you're on the wrong track right now, just be patient and still; you won't stay there for long. Instead of trying to discipline your mind with ill will, fault-finding, guilt, punishment, and fear, use something far more powerful: the beautiful kindness, gentleness, and forgiveness of making peace with life—in short, kindfulness. The longer you live and practice like this, the more pure your heart will become.

This is the path. It's not that hard to follow. You've got the brains—use them. You've got some mindfulness—strengthen it. You've got a natural kindness inside of you—develop it further. You have everything it takes to walk the path of kindfulness.

Why not start now?

About the Author

A monk for over thirty years, Ajahn Brahm is the abbot and spiritual director of the Buddhist Society of Western Australia. He is in demand worldwide as both a spiritual teacher and popular speaker.

His previous books include *Who Ordered This Truckload of Dung; The Art of Disappearing; Mindfulness, Bliss, and Beyond;* and *Don't Worry, Be Grumpy.*

*Also Available
from Ajahn Brahm*

Don't Worry, Be Grumpy
Inspiring Stories for Making the Most of Each Moment

Who Ordered This Truckload of Dung?
Inspiring Stories for Welcoming Life's Difficulties

Mindfulness, Bliss, and Beyond
A Meditator's Handbook
Foreword by Jack Kornfield

The Art of Disappearing
The Buddha's Path to Lasting Joy

What to Read Next
from Wisdom Publications

The Mindful Writer
Noble Truths of the Writing Life
Dinty W. Moore

When the Chocolate Runs Out
Lama Thubten Yeshe

How to Be Happy
Lama Zopa Rinpoche

A Heart Full of Peace
Joseph Goldstein

About Wisdom Publications

Wisdom Publications is the leading publisher of classic and contemporary Buddhist books and practical works on mindfulness. To learn more about us or to explore our other books, please visit our website at wisdompubs.org or contact us at the address below.

Wisdom Publications
199 Elm Street
Somerville, MA 02144 USA

We are a 501(c)(3) organization, and donations in support of our mission are tax deductible.

Wisdom Publications is affiliated with the Foundation for the Preservation of the Mahayana Tradition (FPMT).